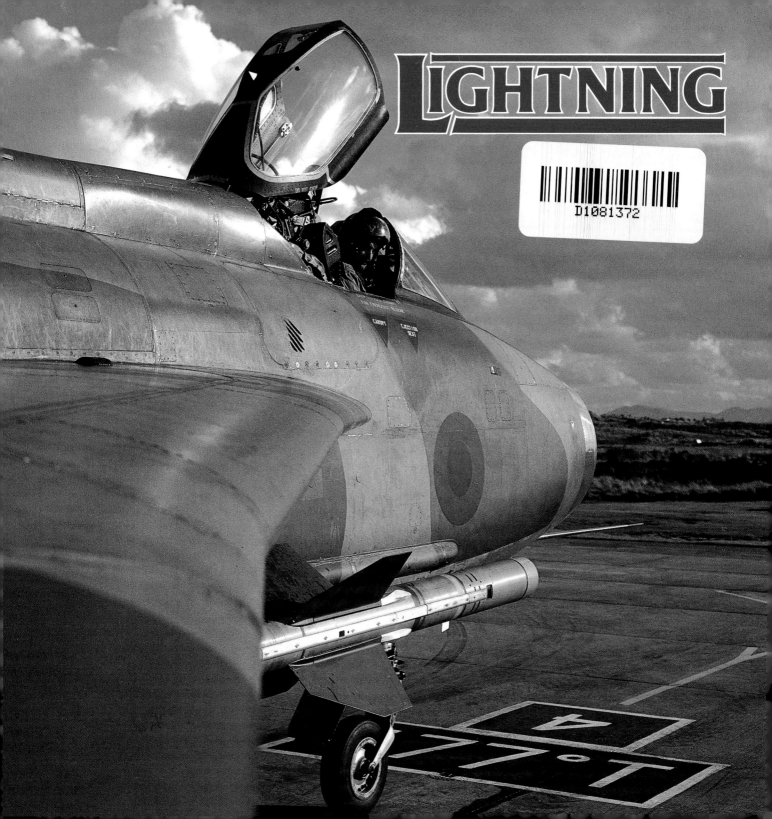

Lightning

LIGHTNING

IAN BLACK

Airlife
England

ACKNOWLEDGEMENTS

'Flying Colours', Jurgen Valley, Richard Wilson, Brian Alchin, John Jackson, Keith Watson and Roger Lindsay.

Particular thanks to Steve Hunt, Bob Bees, Colin Rae, John Carter, Dick Heath and all the other Lightning pilots I've forgotten to mention.

First published 1988
by Airlife Publishing Ltd.

ISBN 1 85310 045 5 Case Bound
ISBN 1 85310 044 7 Paperback

Printed in Singapore by Kyodo Printing Co. (Singapore) Pte. Ltd.

Airlife Publishing Ltd.

7 St. John's Hill, Shrewsbury, England.

INTRODUCTION

Now at the end of its service life, the Lightning has been the mainstay of Britain's air defence from 1960 to 1988. The Lightning was the first supersonic aircraft to be designed and built solely in Britain. From its first flight on 4 August 1954, and for over 30 years, it has remained a classic fighter. Its performance and excellent handling qualities has earned it the affection of a generation of fighter pilots.

Powered by two Rolls Royce Avon engines, the aircraft's acceleration and thrust remained unequalled for many years. With its Ferranti AI23 radar, Red Top or Firestreak missiles and 30mm guns, the Lightning has remained a versatile fighting machine right to the end.

As far back as 1947 the Ministry of Supply issued an experimental requirement number 103 for a limited supersonic research aircraft. Seven years later the original design of W. E. W. Petter took to the air in the hands of Wing Commander R. P. Beamont, English Electric's chief test pilot. The original prototype, the P1A, was powered by a pair of Armstrong Siddeley Sapphire engines rated at 8300lb thrust each. Uniquely, they were staggered one above the other. On 11 August 1954 the P1A became the first British aircraft to exceed Mach 1, the speed of sound, in level flight.

Below: XR728 (JS) belonged to Group Captain John Spencer – hence the code JS. It also carried the old LTF badge on its fin to represent RAF Binbrook.

By November 1956 the P1 had been ordered in quantity by the RAF, and on 4 April 1957 P1B XA847 flew from English Electric's factory at Warton, reaching Mach 1·2 on its maiden flight. By November 1957 Roland Beamont had taken the hand-built P1B to Mach 2·0. Having chosen the name "Lightning" for the P1B (Excalibur had also been considered), production examples entered squadron service with 74 (Tiger) Squadron in June 1960.

Early P1s were excellent flying machines but lacked many of the basic essential items required by an all-weather fighter, the absence of an air-to-air refuelling capability being a prime example. Potentially, had the Lightning been developed to its fullest extent in the early 1960s, it could have become the world's finest interceptor.

By the mid 1960s the final RAF variant, the Mk 6, was entering service, a wholly different aircraft from its predecessor the P1A. The enlarged ventral tank capacity and cambered wings with extended leading edges made the F6 a worthwhile export proposition. The forward section of the ventral tank was designed to be interchangeable with a self-contained gun pack comprising 2 Aden cannon with 120 rounds each of 30mm ammunition. Only British designers would put a gun in front of a fuel tank! Under the cockpit the weapon pack could accommodate a variety of weapons: a pair of guided missiles, 44 2-inch rockets, or even 5 Vinten air-to-ground reconnaissance cameras.

An F1A *XM184* 'A' of 111 Squadron, the personal aircraft of George Black, OC 111 Squadron. The aeroplane is seen in 1964 at USAF Alconbury, displaying its new attractive black and yellow scheme.

Overwing, subsonic, long range jerry tanks could be fitted, giving an extra 4000lb of usable fuel. Underwing hard points outboard of the under-carriage legs could carry 1000lb bombs or Matra SNEB 68mm rockets. This gave the aircraft an air-to-ground capability, a strike reconnaissance role, and its primary air interception role — perhaps the first multi-role combat aircraft. As it was, only Saudi Arabia and Kuwait bought the Lightning.

The Lightning, which has remained in active front line service for more than 25 years, has many unusual and unique design features. Its wings and tailplane swept at 60° give it an almost delta shape when viewed from above. The aircraft's excellent handling qualities are due to a variety of factors: the superb thrust of the Avon engines, the ailerons mounted at the ends of the wings, and its tremendous nose authority at low speed due to its all-moving tailplane. The aircraft handling qualities are as good at 50,000ft as they are at 250ft. In a guns only fight, the Lightning could still make the eyes of "electric jet" pilots water in air combat engagements.

The Lightning's unusual shape stemmed from its design of fuselage mounted engines stacked one above the other. This meant the undercarriage had to be placed in the wings, giving the aircraft its stalky appearance in the approach configuration. With the main gear sweeping back and outwards, the tyres had to be made exceedingly thin to fit flush into the wings.

'Firebird', an F1A of 56 Squadron, shows off its red leading edges to the camera in 1964 prior to displaying at the Farnborough and Paris Air Shows.

The Lightning served with nine operational squadrons in the Royal Air Force and operated from Germany, Cyprus and Singapore as well as the United Kingdom. When the last Lightning has landed, its place will go down alongside other classic British fighters: the Camel, the Gladiator, the Spitfire, the Hurricane, the Meteor and the Hunter; thus ending another chapter in the history of British aviation — "the last of the single-seat fighters".

The photographs in this book are for all those people who've ever flown, serviced, or just watched the most famous British fighter since the Spitfire. Many people have provided me with some of the early shots in the book.

Thank goodness 30 years ago people had the foresight to record their images in colour for future generations to enjoy.

My own personal thanks go to all the pilots who posed their aircraft for the benefit of my camera whilst returning to Binbrook after an arduous sortie. Without them many of the latter pictures would have been impossible.

Opposite: How low can you go? Bob Lightfoot brings his F1A from 226 OCU in for a final low pass during an annual Battle of Britain display.

Below: Formation sunset. An evening sortie for the last Lightnings to leave Cyprus provides a nostalgic photograph.

Opposite: An F1A *XM180* (180) of 65 Squadron, RAF Coltishall, seen in the landing configuration. Air brakes were left out to give a higher power setting on the approach to allow a safe margin for error on landing.

Below: English Electric PI *WG760* basks in the rare sun of a Binbrook Open Day in the early 1980s. First flown in August 1984, the aircraft provided the basis for the final production Lightnings in RAF service. The aeroplane is now in the Cosford Aerospace Museum.

Opposite: After a mere three years' operational service with 74 'Tiger' Squadron, *XM146* was used to train future Lightning pilots at 226 OCU from 1963-1964. It earned a brief escape from the scrapyard in 1964 whilst filling in for 111 Squadron as 'Juliet' before being scrapped at Lyneham in 1966.

Below: *XM135* (135), an F1 with an exciting history, seen here in the more mundane role of a target aircraft belonging to the Leuchars Target Facilities Flight circa 1971. *XM135* had the distinction of being flown accidentally by an engineer carrying out engine runs at the end of Lyneham's runway. None the worse for wear, the aircraft survives to this day in the capable hands of the Imperial War Museum at Duxford.

Overleaf: An F2 *XN768* (S) still wearing the blue fin markings of No. 92 Squadron East India Squadron, known in the early 1960s as the Blue Diamonds, seen here landing on runway 08 at Gütersloh.

Opposite: Half of the Wattisham Wing on the ramp prior to an aerobatic display in 1964. Even the squadron two seater was decked out in full squadron markings and was used in the majority of the shows.

Below: Target Lightning, an F1A used by the Wattisham Flight, seen here at an air show prior to an aerobatics routine. The F1A was preferred as an aerobatics aircraft due to its excellent thrust to weight ratio and improved nose authority using the extra lift generated by the small wings on the Firestreak missiles.

Overleaf: Lightning F2 *XN779* of 19 Squadron, showing evidence of recent recoding, taxies out at Gütersloh in the early 1970s. Along with 29 Squadron, 19 Squadron never adopted coloured fin markings for their aircraft. Only four of the surviving F2s were not converted to F2A standard. 19 and 92 Squadron operated two each for 'general flying duties'.

Opposite: An FIA, *XM183*, of the Binbrook TFF taxies out to act as a supersonic target for one of the resident Mk 6 Squadrons. The aeroplane was retired from service in 1973 and languished on the airfield for 15 years as a decoy before being cut for scrap in 1987/88.

Below: Four from Treble One Practice Formation in the early 1960s, just prior to re-equipping with the more advanced Mk 3 version.

Opposite: 'King Cobra' crossing the famous German canal at the end of Gütersloh's runway. 'A', the 92 Squadron flagship, approaches the threshold at 170 knots. Of all marks of Lightning, the F2A was regarded by those who flew it as the best.

Below: "Pairs landing". Lightning pilots have always prided themselves on their formation skills, and a good pairs landing is no easy task, particularly in bad weather or strong wind. Here a pair of F2As from 92 Squadron sneak over the Gütersloh barrier for an immaculate close formation landing.

Overleaf: *XN781* 'B' of 19 Squadron in the middle of being repainted to suit its new role as a low level air defender. After many years in natural metal finish, Germany Lightnings used in the overland air defence role began to be painted dark green in May 1972 to conceal them whilst carrying out their low combat air patrols on the Osnabrück ridge.

Opposite: After a Ministry of Defence edict in the mid 1960s, all squadron markings had to be made less conspicuous. Here 'L', a newly converted F2A of 92, is towed to the flight line in its least colourful squadron markings.

Below: A relaxation in rules and change in squadron commanders brought back the coloured fins to a few Lightning squadrons. 92 were quick to regain their old blue diamond image.

Opposite: Open top flying isn't quite the same in a Mach 2·0 fighter as in a Tiger Moth. An unusual view of an F2A landing minus its canopy.

Below: With guardsman-like precision, five brand new Mk 3 Lightnings are led by the squadron two seater trainer, a Mk 4 with yellow bands, seen around the Suffolk scenery in a tight formation in the summer of 1965.

Opposite: Plugged in. An early shot of a 29 Squadron F3 *XP700* *(K)* taking on fuel from a 55 Squadron Victor K1. Because of its limited fuel capacity (7,100lbs, about 1000 galls), tanking became a regular feature to all Lightning pilots.

Below: Sortie over, *XP739* rolls to a halt on the Wattisham runway. This aircraft spent its entire life with 111 Squadron.

Opposite: The famous red and white checks of 56 Squadron were the main reason for the hierarchy deciding that flamboyant paint schemes had gone too far. A rare shot of five Mk 3s with coloured tails in line abreast against a superb cumulus backdrop.

Below: A specially marked F3 *XR749 (Q)* of the Lightning Training Flight makes an approach to Binbrook in the summer of June 1986. The aeroplane had been used in Cyprus by 56 Squadron and ended its days with 11 Squadron as a squadron hack.

Overleaf: *XP751* (L) 111 Squadron at Wattisham's annual Battle of Britain display. I had the distinction of flying *XP751* as (DA) of the LTF on its last ever flight. The aircraft caught fire and was badly burned — it proved uneconomic to repair and was duly scrapped.

Opposite: Lightning line-up. 111 Squadron's F3s on display. Different aircraft had very different histories — 'B' *XR712* had always been a rogue aircraft since delivery and crashed after only 145 hours flight time. 'C' *XR713* first flew on 21 October 1964 and made its final flight in April 1987 having served on many units. It's now displayed outside 111 Squadron's HQ at RAF Leuchars.

Below: A late production F Mk 3 'G' of 29 Squadron sits outside its hangar at Wattisham. Many of these aircraft were scrapped prematurely en masse when the Phantom entered RAF service as an air defence fighter in the mid 1970s.

Overleaf: DA *XP741* on return to Binbrook during April 1987, a few weeks before the end of the Lightning training flight.

Opposite: An F3 had the straight wings of the early Lightning, but the enlarged square top fin of later marks. With full top rudder, the pilot holds station with the photoship by knife edging his aircraft to reveal its wing shape.

Below: For the 10th anniversary of the Lightning Training Flight, *XR749* DA was painted in a one-off colour scheme — here seen taxi-ing past a snow covered taxi-way in the winter of 1985.

Overleaf: The view from the right hand seat of the T5 trainer in the middle of a diamond nine formation. On the outside, Ian Hollingworth in *XR753* (BH), and Simon Braithwaite in *XR769* nearest, cross the Akrotiri salt lake at about 2000 feet and 360 knots.

Opposite: Plan form of the Mk 3 displaying its clean uncluttered lines. Armed with a pair of red top missiles, the Mk 3 was unique in that it was never fitted with guns.

Below: After a tour on 23 Squadron, *XP737* was used by the OCU (145 Squadron) to train future Lightning pilots on what to expect. The aeroplane was lost in the Irish Sea after the undercarriage failed to lower in the Valley Circuit. The pilot escaped unharmed.

Overleaf: By the summer of 1987, the days of the Mk 3 Lightning were numbered. Only two were kept flying, *XR716* and *XP741*, for the summer aerobatics season. Sadly, both aircraft were scrapped at the end of October 1987.

Opposite: 19 Squadron's T4 'V' on finals prior to the application of its drab green paint scheme.

Below: Having operated the two seat Javelin for many years, 23 Squadron received its first Lightnings in 1963. Although far superior in performance, the Lightning did lack a two-man crew and four Firestreak missiles.

Overleaf: Flying Officer John Carter shows off *XV328* DU of the LTF whilst returning from a practice interception sortie over the North Sea. At the time the picture was taken the aircraft was actually on the strength of 11 Squadron.

Opposite: 5 Squadron's T5 leaps into the air at the hands of F/L Charlie Chan. Because the Lightning's main undercarriage folds into the main wing, little room was left for fuel tanks, hence the underbelly ventral tank. Normally only cold power was used for take off in the F3 and T5 due to their relatively light weights.

Below: Because of its similarities to the early Lightning, the two Germany Squadrons only operated the T4 variant in the training role. Here 'Q' of 92 Squadron waits for its crew for another bash in the circuit.

Overleaf: During a rehearsal for Binbrook's last open day, nine Lightnings from 5 and 11 Squadrons put up a diamond formation, seen here in silhouette against the sun, and trailing wing tip vortices during a 3G turn almost as if they were using smoke.

Opposite: A well worn T5, *XS452* BT of 11 Squadron, taxies in after an instrument rating sortie. Whereas most aircraft complete this exercise in one sortie, the Lightning required two because of its poor endurance.

Below: A 65 Squadron T4, used by 226 OCU at Coltishall. Similar to single seaters in performance and cockpit layout, the T4 development programme suffered several setbacks, with the loss of the first prototype and the first production aircraft.

Opposite: An 11 Squadron T5 in dirty configuration overshoots from a visual approach. It's easy to see the flaps in the down position from the rear of the aircraft. Each flap was part of the wing and contained about 250lbs (30 galls) of fuel.

Below: Captured by the light, an LTF T5 returns from another radar sortie.

Opposite: The distinctive *XS422* was used for some time by the Empire Test Pilots School at Boscombe Down. It was used primarily to give students a taste of high speed flight and the chance to fly a swept winged fighter. The aircraft was scrapped in August 1987.

Below: This particular T5 was originally used by 56 Squadron in Cyprus, but was left behind when the squadron returned to the UK in 1976. Whilst in Cyprus it obtained a pink fin with flamingo and pink nose bars, earning it the nickname The Pink Panther. On its return to the UK, it burst a tyre on landing and had to be towed unceremoniously back to the hangar.

Opposite: It was some time after the Germany Lightnings were camouflaged that the UK followed suit. Several trial schemes were carried out, overall green and overall grey, before the final grey/green scheme was adopted. *XS452* 'Y' of 11 Squadron was the first UK Lightning to be camouflaged.

Below: Sitting on the Coltishall flight line. this T5 carries the markings of No. 2 (T) Training Squadron, once part of 145 Squadron and 226 OCU.

Opposite: The author climbs aboard Lightning T5 *XS452* whilst on detachment in Cyprus. The two seat variant must have one of the most cramped cockpits of any fighter ever produced, it being only 18 inches wider than its single seat counterpart.

Below: The end of the road for this T5, having spent much of its service life teaching pilots to fly the aircraft. It was reduced to an airfield decoy prior to the closure of RAF Binbrook. All of the decoys were cut up for scrap, a sad end to a once proud fighter.

Overleaf: Air-to-air refuelling with the Victor, probably the most welcome sight to any Lightning pilot. The Victor, itself a design product of the 50s, always gave faithful service to Lightnings, certainly preventing more than the odd flame out!

Opposite: Flown by Flight Lieutenant R. Coleman, a Royal Australian Air Force officer and former Mirage pilot, XS904 BQ, fitted with over wing tanks, now belongs to British Aerospace, Warton, and should fly with them till 1991.

Below: The shape of things to come. XS417 (Z) of 23 Squadron, the 'Red Eagles', lands at Gütersloh in the late 1970s. In the background the new hardened aircraft shelters are easily visible. The white spine is to prevent the Avpin starting system from overheating.

Opposite: Hugging the coastline, a pair of light grey F6s from 11 Squadron fly in close formation past Flamborough Head. The pilot of the nearest aircraft, *XR727* (BH) is now flying F15s on exchange in Tyndal, USA.

Below: The cockpit of a Mk 6 Lightning. Top right corner is the radar rubber boot, stowed to save space, and below the most important gauges showing fuel contents. The centre panel from top to bottom shows strip speed, attitude and heading. Below this was the awkward radio box.

Opposite: 'Exercise Day'. A pair of F6s, *XR725* and *XR726*, armed with live missiles for a 'training day' sit in the afternoon sun at Binbrook.

Below: The business end of a Firestreak missile showing the seeker head behind its glass outer casing. Despite its age, the weapon was extremely reliable, due partly to its simplicity.

Opposite: An early picture of an F6 in barley grey camouflage, complete with toned down markings. This particular aircraft belongs to 5 Squadron and is devoid of all unit markings.

Below: A 23 Squadron F6 at its home base of Leuchars on the east Scottish coast. Squadron markings were similar to those carried by the biplanes of the 1920s, blue and red nose bars and a large white bordered red eagle on the fin.

Opposite: The other missile used by the Lightning was the Red Top infra red missile, seen here on *XR758* (BF) of 11 Squadron during the annual missile camp at RAF Valley. The red protective caps were left on until taxi-ing to prevent damage to the delicate glass heads.

Below: Captured at the end of a hard day's flying, *XS903* waits to be towed into the hangar for post flight servicing. Provided the aircraft remained serviceable it may fly up to five sorties in one day, which for its age was a remarkable achievement.

Overleaf: In the mid 1980s, Lightnings were modified by British Aerospace to increase their fatigue life to keep them in service till 1988. The aircraft nearest the camera (BE) is also having major work carried out on it after the starter exploded, damaging the nose intake.

Opposite: Lightning AE *XR724* of 5 Squadron leaps into the air with two over wing fuel tanks fitted. Not since the Falklands War had these been seen on Lightnings.

Below: The Squadron Commander's aircraft *XR725* BA sits on the Akrotiri flight line ready to be re-armed for another air-to-air gunnery sortie. Each round is dipped into a coloured paint so that you knew which bullet holes belonged to you when the banner returned. Lying next to the bullets, upside down, is the brake parachute pack which fitted beneath the tail.

Opposite: On the line in Cyprus, this aircraft is obviously having problems starting — hence the upper spine panel open, which housed the starter electrics.

Below: British Aerospace's own company Lightning, *XP693*, has spent its entire life flying from the factory aerodrome of Warton in Lancashire. Flown by Mr. Keith Hartley, the aircraft has flown a total of only a thousand hours and is used for development trials with the Tornado F3 and EAP.

Overleaf: *XR725*, once the Squadron Commander's aircraft, on its last sortie before retirement. The mission was a 2 v 2 v 2 combat — two Lightnings, two Hawks and 2 F5Es from the USAFE Aggressor Squadron.

Opposite: AJ *XS933*, an F6 of 5 Squadron, in an unusual dark grey/ light grey colour scheme. Just airborne, the nosewheel always retracted last.

Below: Lightning Leap. Several times a year, UK based squadrons would send pairs of aircraft to Germany for routine cross training. Here 'J' of 56 Squadron, Squadron Leader Clive Mitchell's aircraft, is seen visiting 19 Squadron at Gütersloh, circa 1975.

Overleaf: Having fired his starboard missile, Richard Heath banks *XR754* away from the camera to land at Valley in North Wales. The missile, which scored a direct hit, was fired against a low level flare target in Cardigan Bay.

Opposite: Eagle 1, the Squadron Commander's aircraft, with its distinctive black fin and spine, *XS903* BA.

Below: The first time *XR754* took to the air was on 8 July 1965. Some 4000 flying hours later it was still with 11 Squadron at Binbrook.

Opposite: A few of the last. On a cold December day in 1987, six Lightnings occupy the Binbrook ramp. Twelve months later this picture will be just a memory.

Below: With rain streaming from its wing tip, BA taxies out for another sortie. A true all-weather fighter, the Lightning would fly in some appalling weather conditions, cross winds being the only real limitation on its all-weather capability.

Overleaf: In the bright blue sky 35,000 feet above Mount Snowdon, three Mk 6 Lightnings await their turn for a slot in the Aberporth live firing range. Each aircraft carries two live Red Top missiles.

Opposite: *XR724* AE of 5 Squadron airborne in January 1988. This aircraft was originally built as a Mk 3 but was converted to Mk 6 standard before leaving the Warton factory. Average sortie length with over wing tanks and no in-flight refuelling was 1:30-1:40 minutes.

Below: Moving away from the heat of the Mediterranean to a cold and wet west Welsh coast. A row of 11 Squadron Lightnings, just after a thunderstorm.

Opposite: Three F6s from 11 Squadron in line astern formation show off the aircraft's unique jet pipe assembly. Having one engine mounted vertically above another gave the aircraft its name of 'vertical twin jet'.

Below: *XS904* BQ parked outside a hardened aircraft shelter at Reims, a French air base 80 miles east of Paris. Squadron exchanges normally occur twice a year, allowing pilots to fight against other different types in the NATO inventory.

Opposite: With the massive backdrop of the 'Vulcan' hangar, this photo can only be Akrotiri, Cyprus. Each Air Defence squadron spends 4-6 weeks here per year to practice air-to-air gunnery. The cables connected to the port wing are the ground power supplies used prior to engine start.

Below: *XR754* BC closes up for a photograph similar to those of R. P. Beamont in the first prototypes in 1954.

Overleaf: *XR728* (JS) belonged to Group Captain John Spencer — hence the code JS. It also carried the old LTF badge on its fin to represent RAF Binbrook. This particular aircraft was usually armed with Firestreak missiles in preference to Red Tops.

Opposite: Awaiting the breaker's torch, looking like dead insects, four different marks of Lightning (1, 3, 5 and 6) lie waiting for the scrap man.

Below: Head in the radar tube, this pilot would be looking carefully for his opponent, perhaps 30 miles away and 20,000 feet above him. A normal detection range on another Lightning at medium height was between 20 and 25 miles.

Overleaf: Crossing the coast at 250 feet on a rough sea day. The Lightning's radar, despite its age, could still be used to good effect even against low flying targets.

Opposite: With all its protective covers removed, this aircraft is about to taxi. Canopies were always closed prior to taxi-ing to allow the ground crew a last minute check that canopy/ejector seat interconnections were correct.

Below: An underside view of a T5 shows off its bolt-on refuelling probe and replacement fuel tank. Also just visible is the false canopy painted in silver to confuse an adversary in combat.

Opposite: The most colourful of the later Lightnings was *XR770* AA of 5 Squadron. It began with a red fin and soon obtained a red spine and wing leading edges. The aircraft was transferred to 11 Squadron in January 1988 and repainted in plain Air Defence grey colours and was coded BN.

Below: *XR757* BL, seen landing with its hook down after an in-flight failure. Its pilot, Colin Rae, made a copybook landing, causing no further damage to the aircraft.

Overleaf: A familiar sight to any Lightning pilot — Spurn Point, easily recognisable on radar. It was close to Binbrook and an obvious landmark for recovering to base.

Opposite: Tucked in close line astern, led by BR *XR773,* BH *XR727* and, at the rear, *XS 898* BD.

Below: Sister squadron to 5 at Binbrook was 11, whose 'A' had a black spine and fin, flown here by Flying Officer Marc Ims.

Opposite: Starting the number 2 engine often produced a spectacular sheet of flame from the jet pipe, bringing its temperature from 0°C to 795°C in a few seconds.

Below: 'Shark Mouth'. *XR754* (AE) of 5 Squadron wore some temporary shark mouth markings. Two others were also adorned — *XS903* and *XR770*.

Overleaf: Getting ready for a five-hour sortie, three 11 Squadron Mk 6s about to depart Cyprus to return to the UK. On average each aircraft would in-flight refuel three times on the return journey.

Opposite: Flight Lieutenant John Carter about to taxi in *XS903*. Under his feet is housed the Ferranti AI23 pulse radar, mounted centrally in the air intake. Each radar 'bullet' could be changed in a few hours if a fault was detected by the pilot, one of the few 'quick fix' items of equipment in the aircraft.

Below: Tanking from the Victor's starboard wing hose, 'Hotel' from 11 Squadron fills to full prior to carrying out a practice supersonic interception.

Opposite: Pulling into the vertical at low fuel weight, Lightnings had a 1 to 1 thrust to weight ratio and could easily pull into the vertical from very low airspeed.

Below: *XS897* AC of 5 Squadron breaks over *XR770* on one of the squadron's last sorties prior to disbandment. AC had been painted with the old style roundels to represent one of the squadron's earlier aircraft.

Opposite: Pairs take off in the spring of 1987, flaps down burners in, a pair of 5 Squadron Mk 6s get airborne from runway 03 at Binbrook, the Lightnings last lair.

Below: Representatives from all Binbrook units seen from the 11 Squadron hangar roof. *XS925* AD of 5 Squadron in the over wing tank fit *XR728* JS in the old LTF markings and the unmarked *XR770*, actually BN of 11 Squadron.

Overleaf: Playing follow my leader. Three 11 Squadron F6s show off the variety of colours used by later Lightnings. The leader is in overall dark Indian grey, the middle aircraft in light Air Defence grey, and the rear man in the oldest grey/green camouflage.

Opposite: Close formation, just one of the pilot's many essential skills, used for getting more than one aircraft through cloud simultaneously. *XR756* closes up on his leader, *XR753* BP.

Below: Running through his pre-start checks prior to engine start, the pilot begins the swift process of getting a Lightning airborne.

Opposite: Running through the pre-take off checks only takes a couple of minutes to complete fully. Most pilots add a few vital checks before releasing the brakes however, checking the canopy is locked down, the controls are unrestricted, all warning captions are out, and all his ejector seat safety pins are removed.

Below: Group Captain Spencer banks steeply over cloud-covered Lincolnshire Wolds. It was no accident that his personal aircraft was *XR728,* as on a previous tour as OC 11 Squadron, his aircraft was *XR728* BA.

Overleaf: Showing off the large ventral tank and gun pack, three F6s cruise at high altitude in echelon. The two 30mm Aden cannons were stowed in the forward part of the ventral tank in place of extra fuel. Early Mk 6s did not carry guns.

Opposite: Furz Lloyd and Andy Holmes keep station in their aircraft whilst the T5 manoeuvres into position to capture the last days of 5 Squadron Lightnings.

Below: Having offered to act as target for these two Mk 3s from 5 Squadron, they obliged by posing for a photograph before returning to Binbrook. The nearest (AS) was flown by Squadron Leader Dave Hamilton, now a squadron commander on 11 Tornado Squadron.

Opposite: Showing its upper wing markings and recently replaced rudder, *XR757* (BL) pulls across as the sun sets in the west.

Below: 111 Squadron only operated a small number of Mk 6 Lightnings towards the end of its association with the aircraft. Normally the codes W, X, Y and Z were used on T5 trainers. *XS895* seen here was coded Z, *XR747* was X and *XR752* was Y.

Opposite: Prior to each live firing, the aircraft's weapons system is thoroughly checked out to prevent failure. Here an engineer uses a 'screamer' to check that the missile's infra red seeker head can see the reflected light. The large red guard on *XR725* is to prevent FOD (Foreign Object Damage) whilst the engine is run at high power on the ground.

Below: Still managing to look like a fighter, all that remained of a 29 Squadron F3 in a North Yorkshire scrapyard in 1978. Beneath the cockpit the name Murdo McCloed was stencilled in red and white. Four years later he was to see action as a Sea Harrier pilot in the Falklands War.

Overleaf: Burner break. Executing a max performance burner break in full reheat, both aircraft could easily exceed the 6G limit imposed on the airframe. Although the airframe could withstand much greater strain, the lower limit allowed it to remain in service over 20 years.

Opposite: A shimmering heat haze blurs the 11 Squadron black fin F6 as AA of Squadron starts its Rolls-Royce Avon engines. At idle power, each engine produced more than a Jet Provost's Viper at full power!

Below: As the sun sets on the RAF's last single seat fighter, so ends another chapter in British aviation history.